I0107462

DREAMING OF SUNFLOWERS:

MUSEUM POEMS

Lucille Lang Day

Blue Light Press

WINNER OF THE 2014 BLUE LIGHT POETRY PRIZE
DREAMING OF SUNFLOWERS: MUSEUM POEMS

Copyright © 2015 by **Lucille Lang Day**

All rights reserved. Printed in the United States of America. No part of this book may be used or reproduced in any manner without written permission except in the case of brief quotations embodied in critical articles and reviews.

BOOK AND COVER DESIGN
Melanie Gendron
www.melaniegendron.com

COVER PAINTING
Girasol Dinámico, Copyright © by Ricardo Chávez-Méndez
Artist's website: www.curvismo.com

AUTHOR PHOTO
Hilary Brodey

ISBN: 978-1-4218-3739-0

FIRST PRINTING

BLUE LIGHT PRESS
www.bluelightpress.com
Email: bluelightpress@aol.com

Also by Lucille Lang Day

POETRY
The Curvature of Blue
Infinities
Wild One
Fire in the Garden
Self-Portrait with Hand Microscope

POETRY CHAPBOOKS
God of the Jellyfish
The Book of Answers
Lucille Lang Day: Greatest Hits, 1975–2000

MEMOIR
Married at Fourteen: A True Story

CHILDREN'S BOOK
Chain Letter

SCIENCE EDUCATION
How to Encourage Girls in Math and Science:
Strategies for Parents and Educators (coauthor)

SEEK (Science Exploration, Excitement, and Knowledge):
A Curriculum in Health and Biomedical Science
for Diverse 4th and 5th Grade Students (editor)

Family Health and Science Festival: A SEEK Event (editor)

ACKNOWLEDGMENTS

I am grateful to the editors of the following publications, in which some of the poems have appeared, sometimes in slightly different form:

The Addison Street Anthology (Heyday): "Cell" from "Self-Portraits at the Health Museum"

Arroyo Literary Review: "Clichés from the Caves" and "Falling in Florence"

Berkeley Poets Cooperative: "Quilt"

Ekphrasis: "Pygmalian"

ForPoetry.com: "At Dulles International After Visiting the Holocaust Museum" and "Business in DC"

The Green Door: "The Empire of Lights," "The Two Fridas" and "Water Lilies"

Heavy Bear: "Kahlo Catalog"

Iodine Poetry Journal: "The Lark's Wing, Encircled with Golden Blue, Rejoins the Heart of the Poppy Sleeping on the Diamond-Studded Meadow"

Lips: "Last Day in Amsterdam"

Marin Poetry Center Anthology: "Artists at Chauvet"

Psychological Perspectives: "Evenk Shaman's Costume"

Parthenon West Review: "Visitor"

Poemeleon.org: "What We Missed"

PoetryMagazine.com: "Inside My Eye"

Red Wheelbarrow: "Elegy for the Hall of Health"

Tule Review: "Sleeping in the Ruins"

U.S. 1 Worksheets: "Vincent's Bedroom in Arles"

"Falling in Florence" was nominated for a Pushcart Prize by *Arroyo Literary Review*. "Water Lilies" received First Prize in the 2013 Dancing Poetry Contest of Artists Embassy International.

For my husband Richard,
who explores museums with me,
and for all of the people
who bring history, culture and science to the public
at museums and historical sites

CONTENTS

Behind the Scenes at the Museum

St. Paul, Minnesota

A science museum, big as a factory,
as much underground as above:
wide, white basement hallways,
fabrication rooms, stored collections.
A giant door leads to a gallery
of room-size vaults where temperature,
humidity and light are controlled.

In one, shelves hold jars of creatures
floating in fixative (shrimp,
crabs, mice, fetal mountain goats);
another has drawers of insects
(a huge butterfly with blue, iridescent
wings, a stick bug one foot long
from South America).

A whole vault for dinosaur bones,
another where a bison skeleton
has been assembled, then blessed
by tribal elders. More treasures:
a fossil tortoise, 350,000 years old;
a bald eagle, its white tail
and brown wings spread in a drawer.

Earrings of shiny green beetle wings
and a necklace of small birds
from Peru. From the Plains,
beaded moccasins and dresses.
Samples of corn: miniature ears,
red or brown, more than one hundred
years old, more nutritious and tasty

the curator says, than corn today.
Some corn now exists only here,
but the museum is planting seeds
to give the corn back to the tribes
who gave it to early anthropologists,
who couldn't give them back their land
but at least thought to save the sacred corn.

Business in DC

At thirty-three thousand feet
I think of my ancestors: the one
who yearned for his wife as he tended
the sick the first winter in Plymouth;
the one whipped at the post in 1645
for fornication; the ones who gathered
in the longhouse, wove bulrush mats
for floors of their *wetuash,* and taught
the Pilgrims how to plant maize.

What would they think of this view
of wrinkled hills, quilted farms
and glittering cities? Of cell phones,
email, fax machines and DVDs?
Would they be awed by ice-blue peaks
that rise from twisting river valleys?
Have fun Googling? Be shocked
by the war in Iraq, the Pacific
trash vortex and global warming?

I'd take my great-grandfather
who joined the Union Army in 1863,
at seventeen, to Ford's Theater to see
the single-shot pistol used to kill Lincoln,
the ones who fought the Redcoats
to see the Star-Spangled Banner
at the Smithsonian, its tattered wool
and cotton spread on a table where
conservators work behind glass.

At the Museum of the American Indian
I'd show all of them the baskets

whose designs mean people emerge
from previous worlds to enter this one.
I wish my forebears could gather in DC
for a stomp dance, then visit the National
Museum of Dentistry to contemplate ivory,
gold and asses' molars, all bound together,
in George Washington's false teeth.

At Dulles International After Visiting the Holocaust Museum

After passing security, I settle into a chair
at Gate C28 and cross my feet
on the blue-and-gray industrial carpet.

Eyes concealed by dark glasses,
a gaunt man in loafers skims *Newsweek*.
A wet or hungry baby starts to scream.

A bald man holds a folded paper,
a black man reads a thick gold book,
a boy in Nikes can't sit still.

Studying her boarding pass, a woman
in bright red spike heels looks
impatient, as people wheel luggage

this way and that, each one lucky,
each one blessed. Their shoes will not
molder in piles, coated with ash and dirt.

One of the crowd, I tap my sandaled foot,
taking notes in my little green book.
So many people, rattled or calm,

happy or not, young or old,
going where they want to go. May
it always be. I whisper low, *Godspeed*.

What We Missed

Atoms churning in the nothingness that was everything before planets congealed like cooling candy spheres; tectonic plates grinding against each other, then upthrusting to form mountains like hopes rising against all odds; the first cells to grow in colonies on rocks, unaware of their own shining; the sudden cluster of neurons (a brain!) in a flatworm on the floor of the sea; the stubby legs of the first awkward beings that stumbled onto land; the dinosaur egg that cracked open, releasing a leathery bird into the empty sky; the asteroid that smashed into Earth, filling the air with so much ash and dust that nearly everything died; the first shrewlike creature to suckle its young in a tree; the first hominid who used a stone as a tool to smash another stone; the slow journeys that took people from Africa to Europe, Asia and the Americas, one step at a time, through drought and snow; construction of the temples in Jerusalem, stone by pale stone. We missed the Ice Age, the Stone Age, the Bronze Age, the Iron Age, the Dark Ages, the Renaissance, the Industrial Revolution, the first staging of Hamlet, the *Mayflower's* arrival at Plymouth, Ben Franklin's kite, Edison's first lightbulb, the Wright brothers' flight. We missed it all—even our own births and all the moments of our lives—because we didn't go to the science center at Zilker Park. We stayed in our hotel room in Austin with the two double beds with gargantuan headboards and a view of cars and trucks, going somewhere, anywhere, rushing down I-35, leaving us behind.

EVENK SHAMAN'S COSTUME

musée du quai Branly, Paris

In a glass case, temperature
and light kept low, the headdress
with metal antlers is still,
but the nineteenth-century shaman
who wore it leapt like a reindeer buck
to defend himself among spirits.

The long fringes of his dress swayed
when he stamped with drum and baton
to cure madness, disease and pain.
Let there be magic! A dance
in a sacred grove, to cast evil spirits
from bodies, retrieve stolen souls.

His sleeves billow and stiffen
into wings as he flies over oceans
with spirits of fish and water birds
clanging on his back, noisier
than the families who shuffle
past his costume now and point.

Vincent's Bedroom in Arles

The upstairs room in the yellow house
across the street from the Roman arena
in Arles is almost as he painted it: bowl
and pitcher on a small table, two chairs,
a bed with yellow sheets and a red comforter,
the only difference a second small table
with a box for the artist's brushes and palette.
For a few euros, you can enter this fiction.
The actual corner house that Vincent rented
from Widow Venissac in 1888 was hit
by an Allied bomb, blown into history.

But who can say what's real? The same
Provençal sun warms this house as the one
where he wanted to fill his guest room
with paintings of sunflowers. "I want
to make it into a true artist's house," he wrote.
"Everything—from the chairs to the pictures—
should have character." And if this character
is captured by designers who copied his room
here on a street where he must have walked,
perhaps this is now a true artist's house too,
where one could go mad dreaming of sunflowers.

WATER LILIES

Giverny, France

Pink and yellow, they float
on pads in clusters
forming blue-green mats

Yes, I have entered the painting
to stand on the Japanese bridge
framed by bamboo

a weeping willow
and hanging wisteria, all reflected
in water that's nearly still

The bland gray sky
doesn't matter
nor does my internal weather

Near the pink house
irises are out
in white and purple ruffles

Poppies swish red skirts
like flamenco dancers
I must remember how they sway

Inside, the dining room is yellow
as an egg yolk
the blue-and-white tiled kitchen

lined with copper pots
Japanese prints adorn walls
in almost every room

Like moments repeating in memory
Hokusai's wave rolls forever
its promise unchanged

Last Day in Amsterdam

We make love in our room with fifteen-foot ceilings
and a vinyl Rembrandt behind the bed,
then lunch on leftover sandwiches.
Afterward we buy fusidic acid for pink eye
at the *apotheek* on the corner
and almond cookies at a bakery nearby.

Walking to the Hermitage in chilly May wind
while dappled sunlight pokes
through clouds hanging in low bunches
as they often do here, I keep
my hands deep in my pockets
so my fingertips won't turn white.

The canals—lined with black, red, pink, gray,
brown, and beige brick houses—
glitter everywhere the thin light strikes them.
The paintings at the Hermitage
are by Rubens, van Dyck, Jordaens, and Teniers.
Dancing peasants, witches cooking, and wilted tulips
please me more than biblical figures,
kings and queens, and all the dead fish.

Tomorrow we'll board a train to Paris.
Thin-blade modern windmills—
enough propellers to lift the whole country—
will be turning. Sliced
by irrigation channels, the flat
green landscape will quickly slip by.

I'll remember dodging bicycles
outside the Mellow Yellow Coffeeshop

with its hookah in the window, climbing
steep stairs to the small dark rooms
of Anne Frank's secret annex, and watching
women in bright bikinis with jewels in their navels
beckon from red-light windows while
talking on their cell phones and smiling, maybe
feeling sorry for all the dowdy women in blue jeans
who also do it every day, but don't get paid.

Falling in Florence

I fell in the fall in Florence.
I've also fallen in New York,
Washington, DC, and Oakland,
California. My father and
grandmother had myasthenia
gravis, a disease that causes
muscle weakening and makes
one fall, but I don't think
I have it. Optimism? Denial?
I'm just a clumsy woman,
failing to look where I'm going,
and therefore fell on Via Cavour
in Florence after sharing a quatro
stagione pizza with my husband
at a café on Piazza San Marco
as I was thinking of the *Mocking
of Christ*, a fresco painted by Fra
Angelico in a monastery cell.
It's surreal, though created
in the fifteenth century: Christ,
blindfolded, is surrounded
by four disembodied hands
on a green background. One
holds a stick. There's also
a disembodied male head
in a hat, blowing something
on Christ's face. *Is it water
or spit or words of contempt?*
I wondered. Then I fell.

Clichés from the Caves

Orvieto, Italy

Grind

It was a grind at the old grind
where four donkeys were chained
to the grindstone all day
in a high-ceilinged Etruscan cave
enlarged in the Middle Ages.
They walked in a circle, turning
the heavy stone to crush olives
into oil to be served with bread
baked golden brown as the fields
in autumn, mozzarella, and ripe
tomatoes that tasted of the sun.

Pigeons

The pigeons were pigeonholed
in row upon row of pigeonholes
carved in volcanic rock. The grid
of holes went from floor to ceiling
in caves under the town. Two eggs
every twenty-eight days from each
female pigeon ensured a supply
of birds to be plucked and gutted,
washed in red wine, sprinkled
with sea salt and pepper, then
cooked till their juices gleamed.

Well

All's well that ends well, so long
as no one falls in the well
in the cave, dug more than
two thousand years ago by men
who went up and down it, putting
their feet in holes they'd chiseled
in stone like mountain climbers
today, so there would be water
for warm baths, the potters
at their wheels, and people feasting
on sweet tomatoes and pigeon pie.

SLEEPING IN THE RUINS

A hotel room in Lucca
    painted to resemble
        Roman ruins: crumbling
            stone walls, moss and ferns
        sprouting in cracks

A real marble fireplace
    blends into the scene
        A trompe l'oeil frame
    hangs above the mantel

Breaks in the walls
    reveal olive trees
        and mountains, a domed
    pavilion with columns
        in the distance, everything
            except sky and leaves
        in shades of white, gray and beige

An oriole perches
    on a decaying beam
        traversing the ceiling's blue sky
    dusted with clouds

White chrysanthemums
        bloom on the broken
            terrace painted by the bed
where we wake
        to the rubble and small
            pulse of our lives
        and begin the task
            of saving what remains

Artists at Chauvet

To reach the entrance they plunged
through underbrush and followed
a narrow path obstructed by rocks
and brambles. Once inside they lit
lamps that burned animal fat
to illuminate ceilings and walls.
In a funnel-shaped room where
huge, elklike creatures roamed
on the walls, they built a hearth
to make charcoal, then painted
and carved overlapping animals,
perhaps to show movement or depth.
In one passage they drew four horses,
carefully scraping the stone smooth
beneath each throat. The fourth horse,
outlined in charcoal and filled
with brown, has a dark black line
at the corner of the lips, creating
an expression of surprise. The artist
must have been surprised himself
by its perfection. Recalling it
as he looked down later at the river
and the valley dotted with pines,
he knew his father and mother
had died, his wife would die,
he would die, and their children
would die, but his astonished horse—
galloping through the cave past
stalagmites and stalactites with bison,
aurochs and rhinos—would survive.

The Lark's Wing, Encircled with Golden Blue, Rejoins the Heart of the Poppy Sleeping on the Diamond-Studded Meadow

After a painting at Fundació Joan Miró, Barcelona

The lark's wing: a black oval
floating, buoyed by
a patch of blue sky
small as an inner tube
in the sun's yellow pool

A black band separates
earth from sky below,
the poppy's heart a red dot
beating on a meadow

On another wall
a woman combs her hair
while a little girl skips
past a moon and star

Let the woman skip
with the girl to a place
where the moon sails free
Let the girl find a planet
where stars grow on trees

as my feet rejoin the earth
where the heart
of the poppy sleeps

Pygmalian

After a painting by Paul Delvaux,
Royal Museums of Fine Arts of Belgium

I adore him, though he's gray and cold,
carved in marble, armless and legless.
I wrap my own arms around his neck
and press my nakedness against his torso.

On the ground our shadows embrace
on a field of stones in front of a hillside
where little or nothing grows. Another
naked woman takes a stroll behind me.

A plant sprouts from her head; a flower
floats before her. She is abundance,
a garden. A man in a black hat and coat
hurries by the way men do, doesn't notice.

At least my own man doesn't disappear.
When he wakes, we'll drink Cabernet,
walk down the Champs-Elysées. I snuggle
closer, whisper in his ear; I think he hears.

THE EMPIRE OF LIGHTS

After a painting by René Magritte,
Royal Museums of Fine Arts of Belgium

The daytime sky does not
    illuminate trees
or the green-shuttered house
    reflected in water.

An old-fashioned streetlamp
    gleams against gloom.
It's day and night at the same time,
    summer and winter

in a place where I am both
    a child riding a merry-go-round
and a solitary adult
    gazing at a painting.

Lights come on in two windows.
    Is dawn breaking?
Or is it still night
    under clouds that float

in a commonplace blue sky
    holding back its brightness?

THE TWO FRIDAS

After a painting by Frida Kahlo,
San Francisco Museum of Modern Art

An artery binds the two Fridas:
one whose heart is split open,
revealing chambers like nests
where tiny snakes could hide;
the other with a heart that's whole—
a great ripe fruit on her purple shirt.

The artery sprouts outside
the women's bodies from a photo
of Diego in the left hand of the one
whose heart is whole. The other,
her white dress torn, tries to stanch
the flow of blood onto her skirt.

Conjoined twins bound to one man,
they sit side by side, hand in hand.
The artist can't let either go.

KAHLO CATALOG

Portrait of Alicia Galant
Portrait of Virginia
Self-Portrait
The Bus
Two Women
Self-Portrait
Frida and Diego Rivera
My Birth
Flower of Life
Self-Portrait
My Dress Hangs There
My Nurse and I
The Little Deer
Self-Portrait
Self-Portrait with Curly Hair
Self-Portrait with Cropped Hair
Self-Portrait with Loose Hair
Self-Portrait with Braid
Fulang-Chang and I
The Two Fridas
Magnolias
Self-Portrait
Self-Portrait Dedicated to Leon Trotsky
Self-Portrait Dedicated to Sigmund Firestone
Self-Portrait with Red and Gold Dress
Self-Portrait
Itzcuintli Dog and I

Me and My Parrots
Self-Portrait with Bed
Self-Portrait with Necklace
Self-Portrait with Thorn Necklace and Hummingbird
Self-Portrait
Diego on My Mind
Roots
The Dream
Self-Portrait with Monkey
Self-Portrait with Small Monkey
Self-Portrait with Monkeys
Tree of Hope
Sun and Life
Without Hope
Self-Portrait
Self-Portrait
Self-Portrait

QUILT

Oakland Museum of California

Moving through a tunnel
at tremendous speed, you'll see
a quilt bordered with coffins.
The square in the center
is a cemetery plot; with each
family death a coffin
is moved to the center.
A bright spot at the end.
You'll separate from your body,
meet your friends. You can't
come back if you pass the gate
at the end of the path.
I want to move the coffins
back to the border, push
people back through the gate
and in the center quilt a tree.
I want to make the quilt
where the beggar woman,
bent, covered with sores,
rises from the floor
of the bus depot in Tel Aviv,
young and slender
with thick black hair,
and disappears with her ticket
in the dazzling heat.

Boy at Pinball

For my grandson Brandon,
Pinball Museum, Alameda, California

Blond and brown-eyed, almost nine,
he leans in and tries to hit the flipper
just in time to shoot the ball back
over the waves to the SeaWitch's face
amid the clinks and bells of dozens
of machines lined up at the Pinball Museum.

He's interested but not swept away
by these antiques. The game lacks
the complications of Pokémon, the thrill
of a Skylanders battle, the smack
of a soccer ball, but he braves it long
enough to rack up points on the backbox.

His grandfather, slender and seventeen,
played avidly at Rosie's Diner
while I sat on a round red stool as he
pulled the plunger and steel balls zipped
through the maze, "Poison Ivy" blasting
on the jukebox. He always won a replay.

The boy tries other machines. Red
and green pop bumpers light up
as the ball bounces off them. Bells ring,
points scored. He takes aim but misses
the gobble hole, and the ball careens toward
the drain. Gone, like all teenage dreams.

INSIDE MY EYE

Berkeley Art Museum and Pacific Film Archive

Inside my eye the image of a dancing Buddha
forms upside-down
on the curved surface of my retina.

A sow emerges from her crown.
She wears a garland of shrunken heads.
She is golden and studded with turquoise.

In her right hand she holds
a knife to rid the world of false selves
and things, and in her left,

a skull bowl filled
with blood and guts she would turn
into milk of enlightenment.

The dancing Buddha hangs
from one foot, looking out at the world
through my pupil.

My eyelashes are a forest
of bare tree trunks leaning in wind;
tears pool around flecks of dust

on my cornea, creating a sky alive
with stars that explode into supernovae,
sending photons whizzing

toward my retina, where the Buddha
tilts her head, listening for grace notes
as brightness begins.

VISITOR

Hall of Health, Berkeley, California

The phone rings at the same time
Gordon sticks his red face in my office.
He has thinning red hair, a white mustache and beard.
His large, flaccid body follows
in a sleeveless white tee shirt and loose-fitting jeans.

I need to get a flu shot with my husband
and choose colors for my bedroom and home office.
Gordon had a son with a Japanese woman
when he was in the service,
couldn't get visas to bring them home.

I have six phone calls to make while I eat
my tortilla chips and super burrito.
Addicted to alcohol and Valium, evicted
from his apartment, spurned by women,
he sits down by my desk at the health museum.

Does he think I can help him? All I know
is honey bees have hair on their eyes,
slugs have four noses, and Sir Isaac Newton
invented the cat door. What can I do
for Gordon? I let him use the other phone.

SELF-PORTRAITS AT THE HEALTH MUSEUM

Hall of Health, Berkeley, California

1. *Nervous System*

Miniature lights come on
when you press the red buttons.
One illuminates the brain,
where my cerebrum, purple
as lupine blooming on a sea cliff,
remembers the sounds of bells,
lapping water, gulls circling
over a blue sailboat heading
out on the bay. When sails
fill and the boat tilts, press
another button for the spine,
straight as a mast, relaying
messages as adrenaline zaps
synapses, and the cerebellum,
essential for balance, comes
into play. The peripheral
nervous system flashes madly
as you press the last button
repeatedly, and wanting to tell
the captain something about
the power of love, softly I
confess that I'm afraid.

2. *Circulatory System*

These are the rivers of life:
red arteries carrying oxygen
away from the pulsing fountains
of my heart to valleys, hills

and fields, blue veins flowing
the opposite way, and the lacy
meshwork of rivulets where
nutrients, waste and gases
are exchanged. The heart is
strong and hollow, contracting
and relaxing rhythmically,
its four valves opening
and closing in pairs—lub-dub,
lub-dub. Listening to its beat,
lift the metal handle
to pump a reddish liquid
through transparent chambers
as pressure rises on a gauge.
When arteries clot with fat
or anger or too little love,
the needle jumps, and I am
lost in eroding terrain,
suddenly cold, pale
as winter. Yes, I'm afraid.

3. *Skeletal System*

This is what's most solid
and lasting. When the soft
tissues are gone, this framework,
porous and brittle, will remain,
washed clean of love and anger.
Now slip the head of the femur
smoothly into the cup-shaped
acetabulum of the hipbone,
line up the tibia and fibula
between talus and knee.
As a child, I was a princess
or gypsy on Halloween,

not this matrix of collagen
and calcium salts. I preferred
crowns and beads, but
in the microscope, small
dark cavities for cells
surround central canals
like growth rings of trees,
whether we like it or not.
The marrow cavity is packed
with blood, nerves and fat if
you can say "Trick or treat."

4. *Cell*

Every misconception, foolish
wish, and memory of the sea
begins here, inside a membrane-
bound sac of cytoplasm, where
endoplasmic reticulum forms
channels studded with beads.
The nucleus, round and yellow
as a grapefruit on the display,
is filled with helical DNA
encoding all the faults I got
from my parents—insomnia,
fear of water and elevators,
obsession with details, vanity.
Mitochondria spew out ATP
as proteins grow and fold,
following orders from RNA.
This is the machinery of
the soul, where love arises
as a series of electrical signals
mediated by ions traversing
the membrane, and sometimes
small epiphanies break free.

ELEGY FOR THE HALL OF HEALTH

1974–2009, Berkeley, California

Little museum with the heart that opened
to reveal its inner workings,
the multicolored brain with a cerebrum
fit for a whale, the lung box that showed
what cancer and emphysema
do to breathing, I remember
the field-trip chaperone, a mother,
who threw a full pack of cigarettes
into the trash as she was leaving,
the teenage girl who said, "Now
I think drugs are plain stupid!"
and the many children who promised
to wash their hands before eating
and finish their vegetables from now on.
I've kept a few mementoes:
two human bones, a femur and patella,
extras for the leg bone puzzle;
an artery model clotted with plaque
and filled with red liquid
(lentils, representing red blood cells,
get stuck when you turn it
upside down to let them pass through).
My husband said I was nuts
to keep the artery, which is now
on a bookshelf in my office.
Perhaps I'll take it out to share
at dinner parties. I haven't
told him about the bones.

About the Author

Lucille Lang Day is the author of eight previous poetry collections and chapbooks, including *The Curvature of Blue*, *The Book of Answers*, and *Infinities*. Her first collection, *Self-Portrait with Hand Microscope*, received the Joseph Henry Jackson Award in Literature. She has also published a children's book, *Chain Letter*, and a memoir, *Married at Fourteen: A True Story*, which received a PEN Oakland Josephine Miles Literary Award and was a finalist for the Northern California Book Award in Creative Nonfiction. Her poems, short stories, and essays have appeared widely in magazines and anthologies. She earned her MFA in creative writing at San Francisco State University and her PhD in science/mathematics education at the University of California at Berkeley. The founder and director of a small press, Scarlet Tanager Books, she also served for many years as the director of the Hall of Health, an interactive museum in Berkeley. Her website is http://lucillelangday.com. Twitter: @LucilleLDay.

www.ingramcontent.com/pod-product-compliance
Lightning Source LLC
Chambersburg PA
CBHW051740040426
42447CB00008B/1239